About the Author

Alca H is an Indian writer. She had worked earlier as a computer faculty and teacher and now works as a clerk.

The Eternal Solitude and Other Poems

Alca H

The Eternal Solitude and Other Poems

Olympia Publishers
London

www.olympiapublishers.com
OLYMPIA PAPERBACK EDITION

Copyright © Alca H 2024

The right of Alca H to be identified as the author of
this work has been asserted in accordance with sections 77 and 78 of
the Copyright, Designs and Patents Act 1988.

All Rights Reserved

No reproduction, copy or transmission of this publication
may be made without written permission.
No paragraph of this publication may be reproduced,
copied or transmitted save with the written permission of the publisher,
or in accordance with the provisions
of the Copyright Act 1956 (as amended).

Any person who commits any unauthorised act in relation to
this publication may be liable to criminal
prosecution and civil claims for damage.

A CIP catalogue record for this title is
available from the British Library.

ISBN: 978-1-80074-794-4

This is a work of fiction.
Names, characters, places and incidents originate from the writer's
imagination. Any resemblance to actual persons, living or dead, is
purely coincidental.

First Published in 2024

Olympia Publishers
Tallis House
2 Tallis Street
London
EC4Y 0AB

Printed in Great Britain

Dedication

To Tiago.

Acknowledgements

Above all, I thank God. I thank my parents, grandparents, uncles, and aunts. I thank all my teachers. I thank the Olympia team who worked with me on this project. Thank you. I thank the elders and juniors of my family and work. I thank all my friends! I thank my sister Sachu for encouraging me to publish my work. Thank you, dear! Hugs! My younger brother Achchu and my little daughters Ash and Cind stood with me in all my trials. Heartfelt gratitude to you darlings! I thank my friends, Tiago and Mary, for their kind and inspiring words.

O Holy Mary Magdalene!

If it is a song for my dear departed mother,
Now in Heaven and our green planet Mother Earth,
And our great mothers, Eve and Holy Virgin Mary,
I sing of love and love only!

Countless memories, stories and boons flow to me,
And seemingly incessant tears roll down my cheeks,
And my throat seems to burst with filial love,
Pride, grief, gratitude and veneration.

And I remember Mother Arundhati of the epic too
Who guides the chaste, wise and studious;
And also, the mothers who got abandoned in the jungle
Or on the desert on the caprices of the weak.

Also, I call before me from the calm shrine,
With devotion, the Young Mary of Magdalene.
O Holy Mary of Sainte Baume! I adore thee
And wonder at Your Majesty's charismatic beauty.

Can we just scale those old walks to Jerusalem?
And in a day, I want to feel all those seasons
Of the holy ministry, if you will, may we go
To an ancient unreal temple of memories.

Sitting on these megalithic steps let us feel,
The breeze of the warm day near the shore,
The sands and the rocks of old-trodden ways
Longing to kiss his feet; let us evoke the buried past.

O mother, Mary Magdalene, who are you?
An enigma still unsolved; the key witness,
Saw both the sunset and the everlasting dawn!
Where had you gone after the resurrection?

Dunes, rocks and seashore in a summer nap!
Half erased on the sands there linger still,
Your footsteps mingled with his. Did you ever
Hold his arm when your feet had faltered?

Had he ever stooped to disentangle a bush
From your headdress? Had he ever offered
A flower to you and with the saddest smile told,
"Do thorns exist more than buds?"

Had you ever seen a tide in those eyes when
Your feet had stumbled on some stone and bled?
Had you ever been jealous, feeling less dear
To him than his father who called him back?

Let us chat to my minds fill and till you wish,
And walk by the sea on this moonlit night.
Then I may recount my tales of ashes and tears
And of a doomed love that changed my days.

The winds of unrest still bring fancies, once-
In a while, the murmurs of his kind voice,
Patiently given only for your own keenest ears,
That remoulded you to rise above all and shine.

Even now, the moonlit nights tell tales,
Of your wit and untamed ways of boldness,
Of the calm hours when you grasped the teachings,
And of your plight near the cross: subduing cries.

Taking the essence of those holy sands,
And the fragrance of those ancient wildflowers,
And the brightness from the love-lit moon,
I may also one day portray you in colours.

Fascinated by the beauty of your being,
I try to capture three situations, Mary,
One – near him, loosened flooding Hair,
Tear-full eyes of gratitude, balms of aroma in hands.

Second – sitting on the rocks, hand in hand,
Alone among the crowds; your face and brows
Revealing thoughts, trying to sort out ways
To evade the imminent blackest of the days.

The last one – at the foot of the cross, swollen eyelids,
And drained vacant eyes can be read – helplessly looking
At him and begging to the father for mercy and aid,
And lamenting with Mother Mary till the end.

Then O kind heart! You witnessed the miracle.
Saw him in his triumph over sin and,
You were also lifted from the lowest plane,
To the zenithal heights of glory, wisdom, and love.

I can feel the loss you had suffered – the serene company,
The security, of having the teacher near at hand,
The days and nights of intellectual war with the disciples,
On the existing and the expected worlds, all were gone.

Though humble, how beautiful was life with him!
Busiest days of service, bright nights of moon and lily!
The scent of wildflowers and rose; you followed till
His days end, without forsaking in the hour of need.

My heart trembles at the thought of your distress,
How fast the beads scattered from the thread!
I weep over the momentary chaos of lambs:
Shepherd-less spending the black night at the fields.

But on seeing him you rose from your stupor
And went to the pasture to struggle for the lambs.
While you were away, what whirlwind did steal,
A few leaves of the saga to perplex the future?

O Saint Mary Magdalene! You pursued till the tomb.
Were rich in mercy and had a harvest in abundance.
The luckiest lady! To be the first of the witnesses!
Where had you gone after? Where did you hide?

Were you incessantly weeping for him?
Were you endlessly waiting for him?
Was then reverie only your mirth? Or
Had you been in communion till your death?

For the past few fast hours, I tried to conjure,
But you remained mute, though compassionate.
The sun, here greets us with a smile; time leaps
While we drag and prompts to part us so early.

Gratitude, mercy and love were the essence
Of your soul, which was nourished more,
By the teaching of the Holiest! Bless me, Holy!
With your precious hands which had meted the means.

O Saint Mary of Magdalene, the holiest,
Make me see him for salvation's sake,
Make me kinder and humbler in heart,
Please resurrect me, my soul too in love!

Tree

Though my roots are
Deep under the earth,
And I get nourished, I stretch
My branches to the sun.

I dance serenely with
The warm winds,
In his glare, rustling
The variegated green.

He hard-hearted,
Goes away from me.
I shiver and bend down
And all my leaves fall.

Then he comes back,
Touches with compassion,
I wake up from lethargy:
Slowly open my eyes.

Then I tend to lush green,
And so, he loves me that
Flowers blush as in spring,
In the harshest weather.

Then he again leaves me
Without a parting word,
Or a glance, and I again fall;
As a dried flower to the ground.

I am only a cycle of emotions:
I live, love, pine and die,
And wake again thanks to him,
At his will and kindness.

Waiting

I stand on a gorge,
Waiting for the last
And final signal that calls
Me to the hallows.

I am waiting for you,
To hear your voice,
To listen to your stories,
But will you ever come?

The world still tries to lure
Me to the non-end miseries,
Of a golden cage of slavery
And insults and whatnot.

I turned my mind to a stone,
Stood on the highest rock,
And uttered a "No" and made,
A storm to chafe the enemy.

The Last Agony

Mors Voluntaria or self-designed deaths are
Mostly silent! Why do they want it to be so?
The mobile beeps and vibrates before switching off;
Great sirens go at the end of the work,
Alarms rage on or at the possibility of a fire.
The ambulances roar up, hurting the traffic.

But the enactors of customised deaths,
Do not give a last whistle before the start.
The desperate minds' ash-thrown valleys are
Emptied, of its worldly woes covertly,
Volcano hearts burst open stealthily,
Without screams, succumb to stop at last.

Unrealised hints would have been there.
Not of this world look, aloofness from all,
Incoherent utterings, sloven wanderings,
Frowning face with non-slept vacant eyes.
Sympathy can evade that fall and can hold
Dearly those minds which have just gone astray.

Always we should be vigilant to the mute cries,
If we remain insensitive till the lamentation
Then later, we will crucify ourselves at our consciences:
"He wandered many days and nights, irresolute
And frivolous, we knew nothing, now he lies
Insensitive, forsaking every woe and worry."

If he utters a wail at last, draining his own life!
How horrific will it be if any dying person
Would squeal in a gigantic scream, his anguish,
Over his failure and despair to warn the world;
Showing, undying dreams have been finally put out,
Which had lied like cinders in a snow-covered heart!

Then the world will get punished without a reason.
And die an inner death thinking of its mad run to own
Mirages; thinking we should have acted so and so
And receive in the stead of a friend a vacant space,
And the things he left back: a will or a list of debts,
And some memories – sweet and sad and fading fast.

The Day of Deceit

On the day of deceit,
My rose garden got burned,
With an enormous lightning!

Horizons in every direction,
Harvested only
Smoke and debris.

The sun became charcoal.
The earth froze,
In the wake of a genocide.

In the eve, there had arisen
A non-setting blood red moon
With a yellow Halo.

The only habitable place,
Is the conscience,
Within my soul.

I transformed, into a grey
Stone statue, with tendrils
To restrain you three.

On the day of deceit,
My rose garden got burned
With an enormous lightning!

Do you remember the day?
Amica mea, it was the day
On which you forgot me!

I weep for the loss of our-
Paradise which also had lost
Our everlasting spring!

After the legion's fall
And desertion,
The hill witnessed the suicide!

Do you remember
The date Brutus? On which
You killed yourself.

There was also a day,
When your jealousy had
Stabbed a friend to death.

And did steal the life of
A household and dethroned,
An un-throned leader.

On the next day of the double
Cross, the earth shook,
To cleave rocks and tombs.

Do you remember
The hour Judas? That of deceit?
When you had betrayed Him.

On which your lust,
In the guise of greed
Handed the lively to death.

Nothing ended – then and there,
Began the coronation of
A humble man.

Frail temple, silver and suffering
Have gone. Arose his realm
Over the souls of the kind.

Vow

Years ago, a vow, now forsaken,
Had lied between us. A fatal bond
Forbidding our union till death.
But only you were my world!

I married you secretly and wore
The dust of your feet as *sindoor*
On my head. The bells were coming nearer
And nearer as you said, "Yes I do."

But ill luck severed me from you.
I waited but you never came;
I searched long but never got you;
Infinite space and time separated us.

I wept a lot, prayed and waited.
But everything proved to be in vain.
Hadn't anyone ever counted my tears?
Even you, do not value those beads!

Now we often meet in dreams,
We vainly make an unreal plane:
A pretty foolish world, a hide, an asylum for
A momentary escape from our worlds.

In fact, between our lives lies,
The total mighty chaos of the world,
That cast us in two different directions.
And we hopelessly remain strangers.

For the sake of propriety only,
Let us remain strangers forever.
I take a vow of silence forever and ever;
Do you concede, my dear friend?

Like a little kid playing ashore
With shells, sand moulds and shovel;
I make with patience a fortress of a recluse,
A great wall and a crocodile canal.

Moreover, to divide my place from yours;
In a charm, I bring all the lost languages,
Myths, oceans, dunes, currents and ill luck
Of the world and I take a vow of silence.

All Is Fair

Don't be so cruel, my Love,
Where have you gone?
I miss you a lot.
I remain on your old way,
As a withered flower.
Unless you come and take it,
Will soon be dead,
In this harsh weather.

The morning was beautiful.
Do you remember your dawn,
Of mist and glory?
I was in my crescent phase.
I was waning, I was thin.
I revolved around you in stealth.
And borrowed life and light,
From Your Majesty.

Sky wears a melting scarf,
Of violet, blue and orange.
The ocean is mixing
All these colours a black.
Amazing is the overlapping,
Of the setting sun of your life,
With the full moon
Of my mind. Will it happen again?

You, going in full grandeur,
Only to the mortal eyes.
In adoration, I lean towards you
From the other side.
Before I set forever,
Hold me in full grace,
In your arms; In an eclipse.
Keep me in your shade.

While I begin to sob, asking
If it was real or an illusion,
At the parting of our mere shadows;
You take my hand,
And try to console me,
With a momentary diamond,
In the end as a keepsake;
Till the next summit.

The Eternal Solitude

My solitude and the silence around me broke
By a painful squeal of a bird flying away to a distance.
It ripped my soul with silent thunder. Was it tears,
Or warm blood that gushed forth? I don't know.

Then again peeped in the depressing silence.
Ionic seconds of the vacuum passed without ticking.
In the vast unhearing universe of loneliness,
I remained a bony figure even without a shadow.

Hark, I hear the birds chirping afar, and the barking of
Some neighbour's pet. The cawing crow mourns well,
All delineates to me a pleasant sunny outdoor stir:
A picture like the lost summers of bygone years.

Abruptly the stillness chills! Now I hear no crying crow,
The crow might have flown away somewhere.
The birds chirping and the dog's barking too ceased. Again
silence! All went to a sudden crude untimely stop.

Why hadn't I planted some green flowering plants?
To grow into a grove on this land, to bring fragrance
To these tightly sealed windows and for the lively little
Birds to hop around, perch, fight, sing and roost.

Why hadn't I kept an adamant dog at my door?
Who won't ever hear to leave my side?
And will remember his mommy after her going
And will yearn for her while walking and in his sleep.

Why hadn't I reared a baby, to love me
And mourn my loss when I am gone forever?
And to tell my pleasing tales to eager
Little darling ears of my own blood and lineage.

Hark, the grey honking of a vehicle comes,
Nearing my place, loud and louder it reaches,
Unexpected guest? I have to rise from my bed;
And see if everything is neat here for the visitor.

Never had scattered toys or mislaid boots on the floor;
No coffee mug or working scripts on the mantle,
No ash-filled tray or his Commerce on the table,
But it is very cold here, no hearth is burning!

The vehicle has stopped; why? It has started again
But the sound has changed: Oh no! It is turning away,
Ah! It is going back and the sound fades away,
It has grown tender and surely has reached further away.

Melting and mixing with atmospheric stillness
The sound has gone afar and become blanched in my ears.
Again silence! Alas! Alas! It was none to see the invalid!
And I am in my freezing blanket of loneliness again!

Forlorn, forsaken, forgotten, cuddling to the muddy walls,
Sighing, thinking of the non-visitor I pass the time,
Someone came halfway and has gone, who is unaware
That someone exists down here waiting: A non-entity!

Again, begun the birds! Now in an aerial chorus,
Continuous saga! Melancholic tones! And a nostalgic ache
Awakes in my heart, a drowned memory begins to surface,
What is it? Please wait, let me see! Oh no! Now I get it.

The looping trap of *Deja vu*! Once like a weird nightmare
The Solitude – not the blissful one, alighted on my soul,
The mass of the whole black universe in a nanosecond;
No sound! No light! Only a suffocating cold pressure.

I awoke in a shudder! Felt like being chained by spells
Tears rolled down like beads from a broken string.
I didn't wipe the tears trying to understand the situation,
Had I been asleep? Was it a bad dream? What happened?

I couldn't discern night from the darkness,
Nightmare from the misfortune, the story
From history, deafness from the silence. Why thoughts
Go slow and my memory is so heavily blank?

I got no answers to my anxious questions.
Breathless I lay awake there without movements, then
Curled like a foetus within the clayed sac of silence,
I longed for my mom: her warm hug and solace.

I called my beloved, I called my maid, I screamed
For help – which never I got. There was a ghastly
Blind of ruin alternately closing and clearing
My view— in desperation, I named it Time!

Then I asked the time either to stop or go fast!
To save me from this imprisonment of loneliness.
Suddenly an oracle of doom slapped on my ears!
A revelation about the broken neck of my days.

"Ye no longer exists and belongs nowhere now!
No more space for ye without this crypt—
Owning which you forfeited your past and
Became so frail! At risk even with the ceased time!"

Coup de grace! My thin fingers groped about
Only to see a mere braid of a carcass and a sad soul.
I saw the vision of the coldest black hole slyly waiting,
Weaving its cursed net of call to crumble my soul also.

The truth dawned on me then! And a hasty pastel frost
Soon seized me; When I had only needed a nap,
Someone kindly had put me to sleep for good,
No more time for me! Not even a throb of the heart.

Had it been silent for long? Since ages and ages?
No, the pangs and the tears indicate a fresh wound.
May be the result of my last lingering memories.
My agonised soul wanted to part away from the chains.

Stopping all cries and cares,
Ending all wars and worries,
Discarding this specimen in the vault,
For the endless time to destroy.

It flew away and watched the subject;
The skeleton and shreds of clothes
Yet my soul shrieked to see the tears
Still flowing from the blank sockets of the eyes!

I cried, cried alone and cried aloud,
And my soul returned to the cage of bones,
It pondered over the deceit, grieved for the lost
Then-thought happy life, wealth and connections.

And I murmured to time, "You had done enough,
Are mighty to control the world but I won't fail,
My old sorrows still stand by me and my gone heart
Beats somewhere in this wasted vacant frame."

Then my soul descended and calmly came to rest
There, where once I had a naive heart for the world,
Which had lost its game-winning and had ceased to pulse;
And silently started to forget my fall and slept.

Thus, I remained asleep in the skeleton for the years past,
I awake once in every decade anew: To a non-greeting
Empty day, forgetting everything – anxious, nervous
And complaining and blabbering to no living souls!

The Betrayal

Was it for sure that he
Had betrayed the master?
Did they both have
The same image as the Creator?

Because in my life too
The saviour and the betrayer
Merged so nicely that I can't
Discern the face from the mask!

With a simple wave of a spell,
He put me in a sea of luck to toss.
To win or perish? Only God knows!
I prayed to mete the fairness!

***

Let my situation
Be their pride;
My anger
Their rejoice.

My solitude
Their festivity,
Let them be proud
Winning their heavens.

I retreat my steps; not even
For once, I hesitate.
I move away,
I move on!

Steadily I continue to recede.
On viewing from a distance
I am static:
Waiting for him!

When an ocean of tears
Had rained in torrents,
He saw only
The waves of love!

"You will miss me
When the unburnt wax
Of life will gather
Near the charred wick.

Then the ruin initiates.
And you will be enthroned
As the sole emperor
Of mere and utter wastage.

I had forsaken for you
My world and
I lost my sanity too
To you, cheater.

You took me as a fool.
Pictured me mad.
Tried to rise in status,
By making me slight.

Not any existing tongue
In the world can express
The feeling I had when I got
Abandoned from your life.

Now I leave you,
Loathe you more than
The whole vices
In the world.

For curiosity's sake,
My Lord in heaven
Gave me a hand
To raise above this flood."

The Presence of an Absence

You are not here yet I feel your presence,
Yet, I feel the absence of your presence.
Oh, I feel the absence of your presence,
Yes, I feel the presence of your absence.
In search of moments faded fast away,
I still walk along the banks of lost dreams.
My glances wander to get a glimpse of yours
But you smile at me artfully and vanish.
Feather like my thoughts float to you,
Nearing a place once blest with you, mind
Flies to the past days and I see you.
As a picture painted with pastel hues,
The place and season are still beautiful;
Something blanched is in me: my heart!
A waning moon I miss the hues of your art.

Everything remains the same, captivating:
The alluring blue sky and the silver-white clouds,
The fragrant breeze, fluttering leaves,
Blossoms and butterflies of our garden.
The birds sing cheerfully of freedom.
But you are far away and here I am all alone.

The Fragrant Song

From the depth of the Earth,
I hear a lullaby sung for me.
My mom lies there,
Forsaken by the time.
I, a repenting child
Mourns her loss.
Now remember her,
Care and mercy.
I loved her.
She is gone forever:
Death came to her in sleep.
Had she felt any pain?
No signs more than
Knitted brows
And a thoughtful face, as if
Trying to understand the disturbance.
I still cry and wail like a baby
Calling Mother! Mother!
O God! I was always busy:
Had no time at any time.
Now I have plenty of time,
To repent and to scold myself
For the past neglect of my duty.
In the dreams, she visits me
Happy and still being proud

Of her children.
And I wake up,
In tears, calling
"Mother! Mother!"
And she sings for me
The old fragrant Lullaby,
The sweetest one,
"Don't cry, be brave
My girl! My baby!"

The Burning

It was pitch dark outside,
Only a star high up there.
Very far up in a tarred sky
Like a silver dot on a black cloth.

I, shivering alone in the cold night
Wanted to be near a hearth.
Then my faded eyes could see
Another light burning afar.

Seemed small but it surely
Nearer than the star.
Maybe a torch held high
Or the light from some residence.

I went out there by groping
On the darkness only;
Stumbling on stones
Lest the light be put out.

The star won't extinguish
But the intergalactic travel!
I couldn't reach there to bask
Even if I hadn't lost my wings.

Who poured water jets on me?
In this coldness who stole my coat?
Every plume of mine they had plucked
And had evacuated me from my nest.

My nest, I forgot where it was.
And when was it? No records,
Yesterday or years ago? Was it
An old tale? Or was my plight real?

But I remember the blessings I had:
I used to chatter and tell tales,
I used to smile and laugh aloud,
I used to sing and whistle.

I had a father with a gentle heart,
For a mother love-incarnate,
Fate snatched them and are gone
To the ashes never to return.

My feathers now adorn
The pretender's court.
They painted me dull outward
What was the hue of my plumes?

I, now, only a bulged mass of flesh,
Quivering in the bad luck,
Only trying to save life
With a little partake and rest.

When I neared the place,
Shouts and threats
In angriest tones
Of mixed tongues were heard.

A lot of people there
Near a campfire;
People sitting in rounds,
Some standing in groups.

Getting the warmth;
My eyesight was restored,
My limbs unstiffened,
I felt more living.

I could utter a sound,
Then they saw me.
All hustle went silent,
All eyes stared at me.

Then someone screamed
"It is she! How changed!"
A murmur began and
Reached the former pitch.

Another howled, "She here!
Before the time is due?
How fast! Saved our labour!"
And all laughed and cheered.

"The abhorred thing reached
Here to kill our pleasure."
"Our party not over
And we hadn't our food."

"Dispose of her first
Then we feast."
"Hold her and slay her."
"Kill her and singe her."

***

They are going to burn me alive.
What was my fault?
In my memory spiralled
The shadows of my struggle.

I resisted villainy,
I cried in my agony,
And demanded justice.
But these are not the cause.

Fear of the wisdom
Rising and standing up
To question the system!
The inept power can't bear it.

Jealousy is the double
Edged poisoned sword,
Which hits the slayer before
Butchering the victims.

No other reason is there,
To kill someone
With such prompt action
On false allegations.

Charges read aloud
For the mimed public.
To prevent later scandals
Or adulation of the dead.

Sneered me outlaw?
You! Villainous lover of flesh.
Termed me a traitor?
You! The usurpers' emperor.

Loathed me – witch?
A pretentious irreligious fraud;
Who acts to be modest?
Living in a house of skeletons.

All accusations – false and alike,
They have read their own crimes,
And felt themselves half-purged,
And smiled sighs of satisfaction.

The light I saw was
The fires to burn me,
The pyre to ash me,
Alive.

It can't be averted,
No one to save me,
All those phases are,
Over.

Fearing lest I avenge
All have fled with feet,
Leaving their feast,
Now – under their roofs.

Now I have to face
My fate bravely.
Who is there?
Brutus!

Fortifying the fire!
I know you. In the past
You well scaled
Fairness for silver.

Alas! You too fell!
From what heights?
Now – an executioner,
Forgot your own past?

Now you earn
By killing others.
What a play!
I pity!

But I grin too!
You are not looking at me:
Your mind gone and are picking
The leftovers to Gorge!

With a spade
I am being hurled to the fire,
Not with bloody hands,
It is a solace at last.

In the end,
I want to sing a song of doom.
No sound comes from
My broken neck.

Now I pray,
Or cry in a pathetic voice
O God!
I am ready!

Half killed by apathy,
Now I am dying literally
To a pinch of ash,
But my curse will be alive.

Look! A dark cloud over
The towers hover! In an hour
All will be gone! Look!
 It has got terrible wings!

The Girl from the Past

Dearie, my love of a faded era,
The embodiment of beauty of all my songs,
I behold you in mind now, as I saw you then:
An untimely lilac through the mist.

On that lake, I was sitting alone
In a boat: had forgotten to paddle,
Wondering whether my writings
Had reached that stumbled end.

You were with your friends,
Your team had spent the day
Like fluttering ribbons of the rainbow
Over the lake and on the shore.

You, kids in another boat came near me.
"Writer, we like your poems
And we adore you," screamed
Your friend and you only smiled.

The lake was still like a mirror
And reflected the firmament with no error.
But all the charms of the place
Were enchanted to your face.

Your loveliness had lit the place,
And was naively taking the souls.
By winning the heart of the lake,
Your eyes had made the waves to stop.

In one epoch scaling stare, I wished
To measure the tangent rays of those gems,
By flying your hair over your brow.
The wind tried to ruin my efforts.

And I couldn't make out tears or laugh,
Loneliness or merriment; mercy
Or cold silence lingering there
Which captivated all to a trance.

But those seemed the heavens to which
My songs hoped to aspire.
And the dooms land where my ego
Would like to rest till the unticking of time.

Then your pack rowed away.
The screamer screamed, "See you, sir."
Someone waved to me and you just smiled,
"Is she mute?" to myself I asked.

Then afar from me with your joyous party.
You laughed with eternal happiness,
That slashed my sorrowful mind and
Conscience as by a poisonous dagger.

At last, at dusk when I had retired
To an easy chair by the lake,
And was trying to read you came timidly
And showed me an autograph to sign.

My head seemed frozen to a daze,
I just looked up at askance,
And you uttered your sweet name,
I heard nothing after that, dear!

I wrote, 'To a lilac butterfly' and
Signed and added my address too.
Reading those words, you smiled
And left closing the book.

Then your friends swarmed in;
To get my autograph and to bid goodbye
And gave me flowers and keepsakes,
And went away from my life for good.

I waved to all of you at the departure;
You might have seen a lonely figure
Merging with the coming night there
While you were going to sunny days.

Flash of your beauty in mind
Woke my dead art to life.
Many a poem of mine
Were born there on that hill.

Thus, you evoked the light
Again, in my thoughts.
And by getting a glimpse of you
Treasures began to come to me.

My mind desired to possess you.
Its greed knew no bounds.
It was wanting a signal to start, but
Your unpromised letters never came.

Engraved deeply remained your charm
But not even in dreams I got your presence.
I visualised your golden cage
Where you reclined singing of love.

In revenge, I transformed you,
To me in a song of misty love:
A damned desperate lost soul
Waiting for the deserted lover.

You, young divine beauty!
I made you plain with my magic words,
And painted myself as a blue-eyed
Playboy – a prince of luck.

Whose abusing, avoiding and
Forgetting mien let you wander,
For the whole long years to come,
Among a million horrific shades.

At last, with effort, I triumphed:
I made a dark song of bitter love.
In it, I remained the green of green,
And you grew older line by line.

The song although a short one
Went well read and was on the air
For a little while. I was amused
When I got a humble prize for it!

But my mind yesternight did
An antidote to my efforts and
All my egoic castles and pyramids
In a second were crushed to sand.

I dreamt of you as an angel of life
With snowy twinkling plumes;
Me, a reptile without any grace
Of any of its genus living.

There was a magical background,
Of light hues in the sky,
Waving your wings of tinkling quills,
You sang weaving circles in the air.

Looking from the deep moor
Of clouded muddy water life,
I begged for my redemption
You drew an arc with the wand.

Then I arose to my feet
And became me again.
But you were not to be seen—
 Gone like that dream

O white rose! You unwittingly
Had helped me to regain my gift.
In return what did I do? Tarnished
You as my bonded slave in a song!

Penitent, I sing another song for you.
In which you are a generous fairy
Who gives me alms which muses woo,
To sing till the end, of your Glory.